Psychological Analysis of Confessions by Serial Killers

Psychological Analysis of Confessions by Serial Killers

August Raines

Contents

1

Introduction

Serial killers and true crime have become an increasingly popular topic of fascination among the general public. Television shows such as Mindhunter further help to propel the issue into the forefront of media platforms. While the public is keen to learn about the gruesome crimes themselves and the offenders in general, there is little information on the actual confessions of such individuals. The limited information states that they may be a ruse to confuse authorities or that the criminal may be trying to sway the public. Newspaper articles present either far more extensive crime reports or notes on the sensationalized confessions. However, to better understand why individuals kill, why the crime fascinates others, and to be able to assist during investigations, it is important to explore these given confessions.

Confessions are a powerful form of evidence used in court and for social critique. They have the ability to tell us about the person and hold the suspect accountable for their actions. Furthermore, the confessor must take responsibility and enact their crimes explicitly for strangers, who can then have vicariously lived the offense through their words. This introduces the potential for the listener or reader to identify with the murderer on a personal or human level. Although The Police and Criminal Evidence Act of 1984 now forces the police to videotape all confessions, this evidence is still rooted in the very powerful psychological showing made on behalf of the confessor. This takes the act of confession further than a simple description of the act, showing a mirroring into the psyche of the criminal.

Background and Significance

Many serial killers try to give full confessions, waive their right to appeal, and demand a death penalty sentence. This is because they ethically think they should be executed, as they believe the death penalty applies to cold-hearted murderers, not to them. They consider themselves sane and clever, and they know they have simply executed a death sentence before the rest of society kills them, either through old age or death row mutinies. A depth psychological analysis can verify these ideas, which are often irrational and full of human contradictions.

A full confession is characterized by inmates who are temporarily healed because they make totally honest, sincere, and unfeigned revelations. They finally become terrified at the dipsomaniacal abyss they fall into in their attempts at fake psychiatric amnesia and proficiency in serial murder detection defenses. Here they must dry out in street jargon. While they are physically dry, they try to dry out emotionally too, achieving a total drainlessness when no excuses are necessary in their detailed spontaneous confession.

An effective researcher or therapist is a man or a woman who can perform an essential face-to-face and detailed emotional intelligence social interrogation. Psychologies of mystical contemplation, rational soul, and hands mysticism anger the surviving majority mortified by the death penalty. Ethical analysis enables a "right" of access to the view of their full confessions as part of their acceptance of the death sentence they imposed on themselves. A full confession is produced to avoid possible future death row mutinies against them.

2

Understanding Serial Killers

The term 'serial killer' refers to individuals who, depending on the motive, social background and the climate in which they operate, murder three or more victims with "cooling-off periods". Despite the differing motives and various methods of killing which are used by the aforementioned serial killers, there appears to be a notable similarity in these murderers. It primarily regards the primary motives behind the acts, which typically lead to, for example, fulfillment of sexual needs. The most frequently suggested descriptions of serial killers are the following: 1) Manson's perspective, according to which a "serial killer kills with purpose to find fulfillment, revenge, or simply spontaneity"; Manson explains that modern "Jack the Rippers" get straight to the point, while their "practice develops into a mechanism"; 2) O'Neil's view, describing serial killers as individuals who kill three or more people with a "cooling-off" period for sexual motivation; 3) Stratton's and Bilton's opinions categorizing serial killers under specific types as well as with regard to the purpose which makes them kill other people.

Reproducing a distinct psychological profile of serial killers (because of their unfitness for the treatment scheme which applies to other convicts), the authors hint at six disorders which characterize latent serial killers: 1) oneiromanic disorder; 2) core schizophrenic disorder with paranoia; 3) borderline disorder; 4) affect/psychopathy disorder; 5) dissocial personality disorder/psychopathy; 6) pass-aggressive personality disorder. The reasons for killing are not only vital to the psychopathology but also to the criminal nature of the spoken serial killer. In fact, a thorough analysis of the structure and character of the serial killer's testimony allows a deeper understanding of the personality of the respondent, of the logic of hypocrisy underlying it, and of events the testimony refers to, and finally - to verify the nature of the psychopathological modifications of criminals' personality.

Definition and Characteristics

The term "serial killer" was first used by Robert K. Ressler from the FBI, who had to find a new way of defining these criminals. According to him, a serial killer is "an individual who has killed two or more people in more than a month's time span with a cooling off period between the homicidal incidents". This is still one of the few definitions that is widely accepted by criminologists today.

Another source, the Behavioral Science Unit of the FBI, recognizes four other characteristics that make serial killers so remarkably different from non-serial killers. Their first characteristic is that the primary motive for the crime is psychological. Most of them are motivated by uncontrollable internal psychological processes. Secondly, a serial killer has a cooling-off period after which acting on his inner compulsive need to kill builds up to a new crime. Thirdly, the victim of choice of a serial killer is often completely out of place in their common surroundings. The fetish or fantasy these killers have forces them not to take victims close, or even not to take the risk of rousing suspicion by taking a stranger to some place. Many killers kill nearby prostitutes or otherwise street-active people such as transvestites, the homeless, or runaways. Last but not least, the act of killing is usually carefully planned and the killer mostly aims to cover up the crime beforehand. When profiling murder scenes, these five characteristics must always be kept in mind by investigators.

Honest confessions of what really happened can give both investigative agents and victims' families some kind of closure and can be seen as the first sign of a certain remorse for the crimes committed. These statements create a supposed intimacy between the killer and the reader and are often written in a way that the confessor can voice his displeasure with the court's decision.

The sincerity of these confessions can actually only be assessed by an extensive psychological analysis that would take into account the psychological makeup and social interaction of a killer. Activated brain regions give insight into why a confession is so important to a killer. Evaluated studies on the matter have shown that the emotional brain of a killer is simply part of these shallow emotions the rest of humanity shows when conveying a simple story. Solving a murder case gives an active killer, among other things, a sense of pity, compassion of the interrogator, and great satisfaction in the senses of not only personal growth and self-worth, but also the fact that one is taken seriously and treated as an equal.

However, a killer only reveals what are generally considered substantial situational and conscious behaviors in complete isolation of the actual murder or even entire behavioral categories have been observed in this identification studies. Closely considering eminent personality, the structure of a killer's psyche and subconscious, and manners of socialization is the only way we can even recognize the possibility of a concerning level of remorse in these statements, let alone ascertain the potential sincerity in a John Mancini or a serial killer's confession.

3

Confessions as a Psychological Phenomenon

Confessions by serial killers are a special kind of confessions: the confessions of the most appalling criminals; the confessions of those who have committed not just an occasional transgression but systematically and, in most cases, manifesting the highest degree of cruelty. These confessions contain explicit and incredibly detailed accounts of thousands of transgressions that may be associated with different intentions and conducted in different manners. A very important question that needs to be answered is why would a serial killer decide to make a comprehensive confession?

Each confession is a kind of non-zero-sum game – a process of give and take. Essentially, it consists of a statement transferred from one person to another. This game has no negative-sum outcomes; this is a game in which each person can lose, or both can win, but none can end up being the ultimate loser. This holds for most of the conceptualizations used to date but has not been clearly brought to light. Serial killers are known to possess some form of redeeming qualities such as intelligence, attractiveness, or practical help to society. These may translate to "a chance for redemption" in the criminal's eyes and may serve as the motive to confess to their sins.

Motivations for Confessing

Within the wider framework of psychological analysis of confessions, this subsection is specifically devoted to shedding light on the motivations that drive serial killers to confess to their crimes, the most extreme of criminal behaviors, in order to highlight our knowledge of the underlying psychological processes. A crime confession is generally described as the expression of guilt by an individual who assumes responsibility for criminal activities. The research points out different motivations that may induce a criminal to confess, ranging from a genuine moral attitude to seeking forgiveness and gaining an audience.

When the confession is analyzed in the context of serial killing, it seems that some specific overtones are present in this kind of confession strictly related to the psychopathic personality and criminal behavior. Serial killing is a specific form of criminal behavior characterized by the need for power, control, and dominance. Therefore, the motivation that is expressed in these confessions is not the expression of guilt, or at least not in terms of the fear of moral absence, but rather of the sense of omnipotence and invincibility even before justice itself that characterizes the psychopathic personality, because confession would represent just another means with which to manipulate others to achieve one's own goals. Also, another specific aim of these confessions could be the perception that the crime just committed was not good enough or worth it and that a persona as reputed as the incarcerated person could not have had such a weak prey or a little noticeable crime. These secondary goals closely intertwine with the need of psychopathic attention.

4

Methods of Obtaining Confessions

Methods of obtaining confessions from serial killers and consequences of interrogation: psychological analysis

Confession, as a way of voluntary admission, not only helps to eliminate the root cause of crimes but also provides new knowledge in the field of crime prevention (including all its main factors) in relation to appropriate investigative actions, which can be considered as methods and special methods of investigation. Laws of criminalistics regulate only methods of investigation. Simultaneously, it means that eliminating the physical and social causes of crime through crime prevention during the investigation is not an immediate function but extremely determines the lowest percentage of crimes prevented by law enforcement authorities. The confession, as a method of voluntary admission of criminal responsibility by the criminal themselves, previously developed in criminal proceedings, was formed as a result of the long-term law enforcement practice of the Russian law enforcement authorities.

The following main methods of voluntary self-admission from criminal responsibility are paragraph "a" and "b" of Part 3, Article 41 of the Russian Criminal Procedure Code (hereinafter referred to as the Criminal Procedure Code). The essence of the rules of Part 3 of Article 41 of the Criminal Procedure Code is the recognition of the provisions of the possibility of voluntary self-exemption from criminal liability as the following two mutually complementary procedures and methods of interaction between state body representatives on criminal prosecution directly and directly committed by the offender voluntarily in any form of law enforcement authority (actually the so-called law enforcement authorities authorized by law): from the undercover, express interrogation in the form of the immediate withdrawal of the offender by them for voluntary self-exemption from criminal liability, directly at the scene of the crime; to the secret operations of combined and/or detective staffs of law enforcement agencies with the use of the clearest methods and special methods of investigation in the course of investigative operations.

Interrogation Techniques

In contrast to other serious crime investigations, in the case of a homicide, everyone connected to the case, directly or indirectly, becomes the focus of the investigation. So when potential suspects are completely innocent, they will be interested in doing everything they can to help. But when officers begin to zero in on the real killer, a killer that is often known to the police, interrogation techniques may change. O'Neill stated that, "In addition to the criminal investigative psychology and how the FBI use it, confessions themselves are also interesting to investigate. More specifically, those who obtain confessions are interested in what works."

The psychological dynamic at play in obtaining confessions is complex during interrogations with serial murderers. Generally speaking, the interrogation of a serial murderer follows the same process as the applicable period in the investigation of a war criminal. The objective in both cases is to extract self-incriminating statements or obtain a confession. DeCamp stated that, "A central element of the good-bad frame is the use of techniques and methods designed to make the negotiation process interpersonal." A fundamental principle is rapport-building, an emphasis on relationship-building in the interrogation and needs for mutual respect, rituals, and acts of agreement. This process is directed at disclosing information and overcoming potential resistance, when questioning. Those involved in interrogation should be ready to express their feelings and views about the crime, according to the purpose.

5

Case Studies of Confessions by Notorious Serial Ki

Dennis Rader: Dennis Rader enjoyed taunting the police, the media, and his intended audiences in confessional narratives. The volume of Rader's output allowed him to present various personas. Rader described some communicative acts as letters addressed to a recipient, "Hi, this is Bill. You going out tonight?" Some of the labeled "factor-X" letters were signed using monikers such as "DAS" (Dennis at School), "ER", "BTK" ("Bind, Torture, Kill"). Rader's ability to be playful demonstrates a level of comfort with the activity of confession later in his era of killings. Rader's conception of himself and his relationship to the parties of the confessional act was clearly subject to radical changes over his more than two decades of self-assured killing.

Ted Bundy: Bundy occupied a position of great cultural significance, exemplifying the Bluebeard figure of contemporary serial killing, prior to his execution. Many had attended the trial and Bundy's remarkable confessions at multiple murder scenes. Bundy's many confessional acts begin with a nearly unprecedented confession given in a television documentary. The narratees "you" changed, providing "a demonstration of the mechanics of confession" to the

American public. Volk: Bundy utilized the workings of the mass media to present himself to the authorities, his audience, and to posterity as a mimic, set of mirror images, and an enigmatic puzzle. Once under surveillance, Bundy elaborated on what this encounter has meant to him, how he performed varying degrees of cooperation with the confessional narrative authority, and endeavored to become a benign psycho-cultural figure, a showman. After being found guilty of the face-to-face murders, Bundy described a dark magic requiring his appearance to execute the confession, not making decisions because decisions were made for him, a means of getting at societal issues.

Ted Bundy

Ted Bundy is an infamous serial killer, identified as the suspect for the murders and/or assaults of approximately 35 women from the years 1973-1978. Bundy was initially convicted of one kidnapping and two murders and later, shortly before his death, confessed to a broader range of murders. His case has been the subject of numerous research papers and books. Bundy's life left many unanswered questions and I aim to investigate some of these and more specifically, to provide an analysis of the psychological predicament that Bundy found himself in when he contemplated whether to confess to the many crimes that he had committed. Such a subject matter is unexplored by other academics and not covered in the widely published academic papers and books.

Bundy suffered from a great internal conflict when he consistently considered whether a more far-reaching confession would be a feasible or desirable option. His consideration of "the confession strategy" was instigated by his ongoing profound despondency. Options that Bundy considered were: being beaten to avenge the death of a young girl, "skin" Bundy to discredit feminists, wanting to commit (further) suicide, reconsidering a plan to make a full confession and be executed, making a full confession so as to not escape his life sentence, or alternatively try to escape to make his "head start" work and the option to "escape" by facilitating his coming execution via a full confession. Clearly, this man was entrapped by his own compromise of filth. An interesting consideration is whether Bundy would have the same legion of fans and groupies had Bundy followed through with a confession and had been executed by electric chair.

6

Impact of Confessions on Investigations

Is confession a good evidence? It is an interesting question and its answer is based on both mental and psychological aspects. Clearly, the use of confession evidence is based on how voluntary the confession is. Our judgment is influenced by subjective mental aspects that involve a set of several cognitive biases, stereotypes, and prejudgments. Studies show psychological approaches according to which our confidence in confession can be increased by different factors enhancing the reliability of such evidence.

Studies have shown that people feel more convinced when a suspect confesses out of police custody, when the suspect gives a more detailed confession about the crime, when both the suspect confesses to details about the crime and to the fact that the crime did take place, and if the confession is supported by other evidence. Moreover, the case in which a suspect gives self-incriminating statements will increase the confidence in confession reliability. On the other hand, when those who falsely confess know negative consequences will be temporary, most of those individuals will be able to weigh such adverse consequences against the desired benefits, so long as the desired benefits are of sufficient magnitude.

The importance of confessions increases particularly when there is workable evidence due to a lack of sufficient scientific evidence. For an investigator, the confession of a person in a murder case has a significant impact as palpable proof of his involvement in the crime. There are two sides of a coin; on one side, confessions help the investigating agencies in ascertaining the guilt of a person, whereas, on the other side, faulty and unscrupulous investigation furnishes scope to the real culprit(s) to hoodwink the investigating agencies by introducing dubious and dodgy confessions on the part of innocent culprits.

Confessions are the best pieces of evidence against the person confessing. Crimes want to be pinned, perpetrators want to be proved, and within the system of law, legal provisions have been delineated as state protective and accused protective. The confession of an accomplice could have zero relevance to a trial outcome, but if the defendant does not know, the confession may indeed have jury prejudice against the nonsinging defendant.

Evidentiary Value

To address the evidentiary value of confessions, it is informative to view confessions from the perspective of false confessions. In other words, to what extent do confessions provide new, previously unknown information about a crime? Truth tellers will provide more details about the crime situation than liars will. From both behavioral communication and developmental psychological perspectives, this distinction is seen to be a strong factual substrate distinguishing between tellers of false and true accounts of the crime.

Consequently, a major risk of using confessions as proof of guilt is that subsequent corroboration of the true-crime related information in the confession with that present in the case file adds no new, incriminating information. A genuine offender will provide much more additional true-crime related details than a liar. This means that many details from their confession can be considered valuable for identification purposes. For the purposes of becoming useful as evidence, one new true-crime related detail is sufficient. A liar can, of course, be expected to add some true-crime related correct details. If it were otherwise, their entire autobiographical account would be non-credible and, of course, also not sufficient as evidence of any kind.

7

Ethical Considerations in Analyzing Confessions

When psychological analyses of criminal confessions are conducted, especially confessions by serial killers, there are also some ethical considerations to be dealt with. Whenever multiple appearances of an individual occur and the police investigation has got negative results for quite some time, there is an increasing possibility that the victims will be found in a worse than usual state. To put it more severely: there is a great possibility that the victim has been killed already. In these cases, it is likely the suspect appears on television and in the newspapers with an air of confidence about him, feeling a sort of supreme wisdom not even mythology would dare to describe. But in the penumbra where the dark realms of punishment have merged with conceptions of ethics, despite those, the criminal does show signs of remorse.

These are the so-called confessions. They can describe the details with not even a hint of hesitation or ambiguity and with a thorough richness of sensations. Crime experts, committed intelligent agents, and forensic scholars as well are aware of how difficult it is to deal with people who are hurt, deprived, and insecure. Herein, one must protest. The sensitivity required to discuss or analyze, whenever possible, a criminal confession from a serial killer must be twice as urgent. The parents of the victims have suffered a great emotional loss of part of their own existence, the loss of a goal they sought for themselves; the loss which was to become the adolescent that, in its own turn, would represent the parents themselves. For those who are never able to raise their own children due to murder, there are, furthermore, the countless non-happened existences, the "not becomings" that drown deep in the breast of the grieving unfathered and unmothered. The pure embracement of existence is something destined never to have happened.

Victim and Family Sensitivity

Loss of a loved one can have an extremely traumatic impact on the lives of others. "They too, share the pain." In the eyes of society, serial killers lack a feeling for these horrible losses that they cause. Essentially, because of their actions, they do not deserve to have family members alive nor do they deserve the right for family compensation or loss of pension benefits. On the other hand, the analysis of confessions can have psychological and, especially, ethical consequences. The first and most important rule about the confession of a serial killer should be a certain level of respect or sympathy towards the victim's emotions. Nevertheless, in our study we attended to the psychological dimension of the confession and not to its ethical aspect. The impact of the confession of a killer for the victim's family is of major concern and, on a nonpathological level, should be treated ethically.

Differences also exist in duplicity among the family who love and defend their criminal child or family and those who, on the contrary, condemn him. One way to control this effect of this one additional source of information based on an ongoing collection of data on families and/or direct victims of the murderer that are in contact with our team is to systematically collect the feelings of victims and their families concerning the murderer's confession. There is also a reciprocal effect of the confession and trial. On one hand, a confession at the time of trial favors a lighter sentence. In exchange for such a reduced sentence, the police develop the art of obtaining confession without any evidence of a specific event.

8

Comparative Analysis of Confessions Across Differe

M any of the identified qualitative studies focus on an analysis of interview statements given by serial killers. It is difficult to conduct this on a group comparison basis as low numbers of spontaneous confessions by killers are typically either single homicides, vehicular manslaughters or homicides during crime scenes. An intriguing comparison appears to be a logical analysis of the statement evidence of spree killers in contrast to both the ones of serial killers and those of fourth-degree murder offenders.

Psychological synopsis of the empirical literature according to suspect category. The study allowed for a deep timeless psychological examination of murder confessions available from suspects' statements and their putative psyche. In order to provide a psychological comparison of confessions by serial killers and spree killers, we started with an in-depth exploration of a possible psychological comparison between their two offender groups, as compared with other sufficiently studied suspects, namely, sexual offenders and fourth-degree murderers, as far as spontaneous confessions are concerned. Although it is difficult to apprehend and ascertain the distinct individual or group psychology of either type of offender, based on their offense class, more essential rather than exclusive trends should be sought in distinguishing them from other offenders as well as defining individual and typological differences.

Serial Killers vs. Spree Killers

Both types of offenders confess to their crimes during police interrogation as a rule, and nothing particular is needed to elicit a confession from them. Serial killers, however, explain that they did not want to get caught. In fact, some serial killers seem to be proud of their crimes; they even boast about their viciousness. However, spree killers often get arrested or decide to commit suicide after committing the violent acts. They may believe that they will be killed by the police or they are confident that they will ultimately be executed, but they regard this outcome as secondary or inevitable. They confess to the police their motives, plans, and sometimes the problems they encountered during their criminal activities. Interestingly, some spree killers "detoxify" their reputation. Rückert observes that spree killers decide to call the police because they have made the decision to kill themselves when they called. In other words, their motives are despair and an unwillingness to continue life once they have terminated the lives of others, despite the riot of digital and other related phenomena associated with the deed.

Most serial killers seem to be of completely average intelligence as measured by IQ scores. Conversely, spree killers are not always of "low" intelligence, but they completely lack perceptiveness, and they especially lack the ability to benefit from relating to others. Serial killers, by contrast, deceive people and often possess considerable manipulation skills. This is a critical difference between the two types of killers. Serial killers deceive their surroundings because they do not stand out in terms of their behavior and style of life. Moreover, they are sure that they will not be arrested for their crimes.

9

The Role of Confessions in Criminal Profiling

The confessions of serial killers can provide valuable insight in the area of criminal profiling. Criminal profilers examine criminal actions, including such behaviors as modus operandi and "signature," to reveal the "unique aspects of a specific crime." Understanding the unique crime and criminal through crime scene analysis, particularly by insight garnered from confessions, increases the chance of finding an "unknown" or elusive killer. Confessions offer insight as to "how the criminal thinks" about his offense, as well as presenting information about the behavior and emotions of the offender; a utility confirmed in analysis of over one hundred actual cases. The value of a confession from a profiler's point of view, according to another group of criminal profilers and law enforcement, is founded in the "display of the degree of psychopathy, psychopathology or personality disorder, the offender's normal coping strategies and level of pressures in the offender's life."

Acting collectively, these aspects provide a great psychological foundation in investigating crimes. Confessions can provide valuable insight into the psychological profile of the actual offender. As will be further detailed in this paper, confessions offer a look into the mental and emotional state of the offender. It provides clues to the emotional and psychological state of the offender during the crime and it can give insight as to their perception of the crime. The types of crimes that we are examining have often only one perpetrator, and although there are different roles, there are likely to be only one offender. This person, if they are a confessed serial killer or a confessed murderer, can provide a unique understanding of how he perceived the crime, what were his motivations, what was his perception of the victim, and how he perceives himself.

Behavioral Analysis

Behavioral Analysis: One of the main reasons investigative inquiry series on various serial homicide cases may focus on confessions is that confessions are becoming a common topic of empirical studies. The main reason for this is that a large number of individuals actually disclose hands-on experience in confessions. Based on this empirical research, one could argue that the offender's behavior is expressed in confession statements. But, are these offenders actually giving us insight into their actual behavior, or what they actually did? The belief that a confession is tied to the behavior of a serial offender assumes that offenders are disclosing their hands-on experience, not just knowledge of a crime other than their own.

It assumes that confession behavior reflects real-life behavior. But offenders engage in artificial behaviors in investigations more than just in confessions. For instance, in Japan, police officers are taught to testify formally about confessions, and as such, "problems relating to whether the confession was genuine are not dealt with in court". Culture and society can dictate behavior, and even though the legal process is transparent about false confessions, this does not remove the motivation for covertness from the minds of suspects. There are many explanations for why serial offenders may give false confessions to acts they did not commit themselves, but it can range from delusional systems, intentional manipulation and damage control, to coercive interrogation. Conclusions about the behavior of serial offenders or other violent offenders cannot be derived from confessions, and any attempt to do so may miss the point.

10

Psychological Theories Explaining Confessions by S

There have been very few studies that have attempted to explain why serial killers confess. In their research, Norris and Sorsdev give only a very general explanation and Carson compiled empirical data without any additional explanation. Although Carson suggested that some serial killers do not confess or make nonsense confessions, the same confusion exists for them: Why that confession and not another? The following psychological theories may offer some basic answers to these questions. Although the authors do not necessarily think that all communication is a projection or "secondary gain," these theories may help to guide future research as to when this may be more likely to hold true, indicating those behavior profiles that may offer the most temptation for this kind of speculation.

The thematic apperception test (TAT) relies on the fact that individuals tend to project their psychological needs onto incomplete sentences or incomplete stories, so that questions involving the patient's emotional responses to those incomplete stories may be reflective of the patient's unconscious thoughts and feelings. In confessions, this perspective might be altered so that the criminal's constellation of internally organized semantics might stimulate an unspoken need for expressing and sharing the complexity of his or her own personal logic, in much the same way as the art of the ancient psychopath stimulated the demonic visions of van Gogh or Goya. Thus, perhaps in the solitary world of the sexual psychopath, this "cry in the wilderness" rationale might be considered as an engine of so many explicit narratives. Such a cry could be a desperate need to validate cognitions and objectives against a society that had no fact manufactured to frame his or her desires. Such an answer could also be a wailing despair in the void of a hollow soul no longer part of its creator.

Catharsis Theory

Within psychology, catharsis is the purification and purging of the mind or soul through the evocation of pity and fear, an ending technically known by the term katharsis (catharsis). This theory comes to us from Aristotle in his famous "Poetics," but it is a Hippocratic term at first. In the field of psychology, descriptively it was considered as part of Freud's one-on-one therapy and proscriptively as part to do with antiacting of aggression either as an end in itself or as a precursor to more therapeutic treatments. Unfortunately, any good empirical evidence for this theory is very difficult to find. To make matters worse, catharsis is associated with acting out of aggression; and to the public people are considered to have laid to rest various emotional states usually suppressed within as the result of therapy or an unfortunate event or being so-called cleansed by a confessional.

Because of this public belief, it has been assumed that by Type II serial killers that are sexually motivated (atherosclerosis) and are the more common type of serial killer, that they are motivated to rid themselves of their wrath by catharsis and the killings of each additional victim results in a cathartic release of anger but for a short moment of time. The killers confess in hope of purging their soul in the public eye; earlier confessions were public with confession letters given to newspapers, confessed confession letters over radio programmes, TV, and books. The fame role was an added benefit. They answer questions and tell who they are, as they want to be seen for what they have done as more than what was the killer of the monster they killed. By ridding their souls by their confessions they are more than sated with a feeling of wanting to talk always in mass amounts about ideations of sexual acts on their victims in detail.

11

The Influence of Media and Public Perception on Co

Press releases and media propaganda can strongly influence the motivation and volume of confessions. Initially, an individual might feel psychologically uncomfortable with confession, as one will become the primary actor of one's crime in front of both the victims and society. With this effect, the killer will become afraid of achieving such a state in front of the family and friends. But in general, these sad feelings hardly affect the killers. Meanwhile, the fear directed towards the family, loved ones, and one's own future greatly discourages killers from confessions necessary to escape.

Direct publicity can also alert a killer to the existence of traces or the potentiality of identifying oneself. But more importantly, extensive media propaganda may create a perception in the mind of a lonely, late-troubled murderer who claims to be lonely and misunderstood. Intense interest in the case will help him to spice up daily life, add excitement, and express his fame in a society where it has no value in other areas. Moreover, the harsh press and the police may create anger and help network with other isolated people who are far away from associating with similar interests. "You did what you wanted, but both agreed." Making a confession is to restore power.

If a killer is hiding something and he is very busy, then confession which is not based on the logic of remorse is power done through the public.

Portrayal in True Crime Shows

Regarding confessions to crime and the psychological dynamics related to it, the presentation of a number of serial killers and murderers in documentary shows or podcasts often appears as something confessional. However, the degree to which they can be perceived as somehow sincere or genuine in these cases is contested among researchers. This article advances that discussion and fills the gap based on serial killers' own perceptions of what confessing feels like to them. Special attention is devoted to self-disclosure (or, conversely, various levels of concealment) of motives or mind-state that often creeps into recollected biographies and is often evinced in true-crime-show narrative.

Authors suggest that true crime shows do have some psychological effects that may promote confessional moves in some criminal species or motivated conditions, especially those related to self-presentation, self-vindication, or agenda-pushing, as honesty and sincere confession of "emotional realities" become instrumental to more important·self-presentational aims. The present article, then, is conceptual in its focus. Its aim is to understand the psychological factors that promote script-based confessions in the context of the type of portrayal encountered in the British or the American "confessional" serial-killer documentary. In order to explore the confessional presentation in these areas, as well as the confession of crime material in particular, the concept of self-disclosure and its conceptual frame will be explored to determine the potentiality of appeal inherent in the show which motivates couch-confessional moves.

12

Future Directions in Research on Confessions by Se

The preceding chapters in this book afford the reader an opportunity to not only witness the development of offender profiling and link analysis of serial real crimes but also to deconstruct the complexities of some offenders and their confessions. Exploring and examining the nature of the confessions of killers and attempted killers provides us an intimate lens with which to understand what these criminals are truly capable of. In other words, what is made clear is the least these offenders are capable of in their crimes as all that they have told us is only an account of what they feel guilty about.

When one reviews the literature concerning the types of violence attended to by psychologists and mental health professionals, it becomes immediately apparent that there is a significant dearth in this literary area. The primitive understanding and sophistication in forensic sciences only allows research to date to be fitting of the means available. Research in the domain of forensic psychology has similarly grown in promising ways, yet it has been slow to apply insights from work on eyewitness testimony and jury behavior more generally to vie a consideration of the development of the utility of confessions by serial killers as dangerous to themselves. We deem not to delve any deeper into this sub-area as it is one promised for the broadening of perspectives and a flood of detailed accounts on the ground in the coming years.

Advancements in Forensic Psychology

As previous research has illustrated, there are a myriad of additional variables that may be at play concerning confessions by serial offenders. Some of the future directions for research have identified that there is possible potential in the advancement of forensic psychology. Specifically, an area known as offender profiling is one that has already yielded a significant amount of valid information concerning the habits, characteristics, and possible reasons for offenses being committed. Specifically, psychological autopsies not only benefit from the same information gathered in conventional case studies but also have an abundance of highly valued quantitative data available to the researchers. Techniques such as these, especially when used in conjunction with one another, can help further our knowledge in the area of low base-rate crime, as well as other areas such as missing and returned persons, in which fraudulent claims have not only been made, yet would be nearly impossible to investigate.

This would regard the general and overall psychological and mental health of the serial killer. For one, recent advances in psychology and other fields have suggested significant problems related to the mental illness, attitudes, and actions of individuals with Orphan, as indicated by previous research. Although asphyxiation has been done to great success with this condition, the concept as it applies to homicide is relatively under-researched. While it does not seem that hostage takers would necessarily present with traits of Orphan, the mental states that are created by some hostage situations push the captive-captive relationship more in the direction of an orphan state.

With respect to Exile, it has been previously argued that the popular stereotype of the pathehim tr (serial killer) as a slinking sexual predator who hides in the bushes to blindside his victims is mostly contrived and not representative of most serial killers.

13

Conclusion

Confessions by serial offenders present significant insight into the behavior of these individuals, as well as into the crimes they committed. But given the complexity of the crimes and the individuals who commit them, caution must be exercised when interpreting these documents. The extent to which confessions are reliable or true may be in question. A psychological exploration of a body of extended confessions could help improve our understanding of these complex interpersonal phenomena.

The existing medical and psychological literature in this specific area is emaciated and filled with appeals for further study in order to improve research practice. This interdisciplinary investigation is step 1. We believe, from our psychoanalytic standpoint, that the first step in the examination of serial killers' confessions is the exploration of their content rather than the intentions of the offenders who compiled them. By attending to the content of these confessions, if a psychological pattern emerges from the material, the temptation of the nurture vs. nature question may be avoided, with the focus falling on what a series of individual murders may mean for the toll taken on the individual perpetrating them. Rather than being drawn into a determinist debate which locates the serial motive as originating in the body or the mind of the offender, psychological insight may be offered by an affective exploration of the nature and quality of the impulse behind each individual act. Research in the area will need to proceed cautiously and with a great deal of sensitivity in order to carry as minimal a risk of harm to practitioners or the lay public as possible.